I0558175

SONG OF DERMOT AND THE EARL

Translated by: G.H.C. Orpen
Edited by: D.P Curtin

Dalcassian
Publishing
Company

PHILADELPHIA, PA

Library of Congress Cataloging-in-Publication Data

By his own interpreter
Who told to me the history of him,
Of which I here make record.
This man was Morice Regan,

Face to face he spake to him
Who related this geste:
The history of him he showed me.
This Morice was interpreter
To King Dermot, who loved him much.

Here I shall leave off about the bachelor,
About King Dermot I will tell you.
In Ireland, at this day,
There was no more worthy king:
Very rich and powerful he was;

He loved the generous, he hated the mean.
He by his power
Had taken and conquered
O'Neil and Meath in his war;
Hostages he brought to Leinster:

He brought with him O'Carroll,
The son of the king of Uriel.
Now in Leath-Cuinn there was a king,
O'Rourke he was called in Irish,
In Tirbrun, the barren, he dwelt,

A waste and woody land.
But O'Rourke, the rich king,
Had a beautiful wife at this time,
The daughter of King Melaghlin
To whom Meath was suject.

Melaghlin was lord of Meath;
Whoever would tell you the truth,
She was of the stock
Of the good old Melaghlin;
He was sprung from the lineage

Of Melaghlin of the bold heart,
The son of Coleman, the rich king,
Who was so well-bred and courteous.
About Melaghlin I will leave off,
About King Dermot I will tell.

Dermot, king of Leinster,
Whom this lady loved so much,
Made pretence to her of loving,
While he did not love her at all,
But only wished to the utmost of his power

To avenge, if he could, the great shame
Which the men of Leath-Cuinn wrought of old
On the men of Leath-Mogha in his territory.
King Dermot often sent word
To the lady whom he so loved—

By letter and by messenger,
Often did the king send word
That she was altogether, in truth,
The thing in the world that he most loved;
Thus he besought her very often

For her true love covertly.
And the lady sent him word
By a secret messenger
That she would do all his will:
To the king who is so renowned

She returns answer again,
Both by word of mouth and by letter,
That he should come for her in such manner
With all the host of Leinster
And by force and by war

Should carry her away with him from the land;
That she would let King Dermot know
In what place he should take her
Where she should be in concealment,
That he might freely carry her off:

In what place, in short, she should be
Where he might freely carry her off.
The king summoned speedily
All his men throughout Leinster,
To come to him without delay

From Ossory and from Leinster;
And he let them all know
That he wished to go against Leath-Cuinn,
To avenge, if he could, the shame
Which these men wrought of yore;

The shame which they had wrought of yore
In Leath-Mogha, in his territory.
Promptly they came
At the king's command.
When all were assembled,

Against Leath-Cuinn they turned straightway;
Night and day they marched forward
Rich and poor, small and great.
Why should I go on telling you more?
Into Tirbrun came the valiant king.

Now the lady had sent word
To King Dermot where she was,
That he should come with his men
And promptly carry her off
King Dermot immediately

Came marching to the place
Where the lady had sent word.
That she would be ready.
In this way Dermot the king
Carried off the lady at this time.

O Rourke bitterly complained
For his wife whom he had lost;
While he offered very fierce battle
To the men of Leinster.
But, my lords, King Dermot

Then brought the lady away with him,
Nor ever ceased marching
From thence to the midst of Hy Kinsellagh.
And the lady for a good long time
Was there, as people say:

At Ferns she was placed for her abode,
As people say, in this manner.
O Rourke, much grieving,
To Connaught went in all haste.
To the king of Connaught he relates all;

Bitterly he complains of the shame,
How the king of Leinster
Came upon him in such manner,
Took his wife by force from him,
And placed her at Ferns for her abode.

To the king of Connaught of the outrage
Bitterly he complains, and of the injury;
Very earnestly he besought him
To make ready for him
Some of his household and of his men

So that he could avenge his shame.
The king of Connaught sent word
To the king of Ossory, in the first place,
That he should not fail their king
But should come to their aid.

And these men fully promised him
That they would make him king in that territory
If they could cast out of it
King Dermot who was so bold.
And this man immediately revolted

Against his lord, King Dermot;
And Melaghlin, the traitor,
Abandoned his lord;
And Mac Torkil of Dublin
Abandoned his lord at this moment.

There joined in the treason
Murrough O'Brien, an evil rebel,
Whom the dogs devoured,
As the song will tell you
As soon as we shall complete it for you

Further on in your story.
When Dermot the noble king,
Who was of so much worth,
Saw that they had failed him
Gossips, kinsmen, and friends,

One day King Dermot took horse
And brought with him some of his men,
And went to seek the rebel O'Brien;
He wished to parley with him in secret.
O'Brien, however, kept avoiding the king:

With him he would not, either much or little,
Parley or counsel aught
Nor assistance give his lord.
When king Dermot saw this
That he could not parley with the rebel,

The king immediately turned back
Straight to the city of Ferns.
At Ferns the king abode
At an abbey that was there
Of Saint Mary the Queen,

Glorious lady and Virgin.
Then the king devised
A trick that he would play;
How he might find the rebel
And by cunning speak to him.

To the Abbot the king sent word,
That he should lend him a cope,
A cope for a canon
Or for a priest or for a monk.
To Knoth then the king goes

This time with the cope.
At a dun of his he found him,
As it was related to me.
The king put on the cope
Which trailed down to his feet,

So that one could not but take him
For a Monk Regular.
When the Palmer had come
Before the traitor's house,
The rebel, when he saw the king, straightway

Hurried off towards the forest;
For the wicked traitor
Did not wish to recognise him as his lord.
The rebel then shouts
In a loud and strong voice:—

'Wicked king, what do you seek?
Be off with you at my bidding;
And if you do not do so speedily
I shall have you strung up to the wind.'
When the king heard him,

He was full of grief and wrath.
The king was in great distress
For the saying of the traitor
Who had so menaced him
And would string him up to the wind.

The rich king returned
Who was so liberal and courteous,
Since the traitor revolted
Against his rightful lord.
All his men failed him

Both of Leinster and of Ossory.
When Dermot the king perceived
That he was betrayed at this time:—
His own men failed him
So completely was he betrayed—

And that they wished to take him
To hand him over and sell him to O'Rourke,
While the king of Connaught on the other hand
Should make a great destruction of him—
Why should I delay you

From your geste at all?
His people by the strong hand
Have cast out King Dermot,
Have wrested the whole kingdom from him
And have driven him from Ireland.
When the king was exiled

He took ship at Corkeran;
When the king was abandoned
At Corkeran he took ship;
At Corkeran he put to sea,

Auliffe O'Kinad he brought with him,
With him the rich king brought
And more than sixty three.
The rich king had the wind
Fine and fair to his desire:

His ships had a very fair breeze;
At Bristol they take the shore.
At the house of Robert Harding,
Near to St Austin's,
King Dermot abode

With as many men as he had.
According to common report,
The queen was there also.
When the king had stayed
At Bristol as long as he pleased,

He had his knights summoned,
He resolved to go to Normandy
To hold parley with King Henry
Of England, the powerful.
For the king of England

Was, my lords, at that time
In Normandy on account of his war,
On account of the war with the French.
So much did Dermot accomplish
By his journeyings and so far go

That he landed in Normandy,
According to the old people.
It is well, my lords, that I should tell you
How Dermot goes through Normandy:
To seek King Henry then he goes

Up and down, forwards and back;
He sent messages and made enquiries
Until he found King Henry;
At a city he found him
Of which he was called lord.

King Dermot, as soon as he could,
Went indeed towards the court:
Towards the court step by step
He went away very quickly
To hold parley with the English king,

Who was so rich and so bold.
When Dermot, the valiant king,
Before King Henry
Had come at this time,
Before the English king,

Very courteously he saluted him
Fairly and finely before his men:
'May God who dwells on high
Guard and save you, King Henry,
And give you also

Heart and courage and will
To avenge my shame and my misfortune
That my own people have brought upon me!>
Hear, noble king Henry,
Whence I was born, of what country.

Of Ireland I was born a lord,
In Ireland acknowledged king;
But wrongfully my own people
Have cast me out of my kingdom.
To you I come to make plaint, good sire,

In the presence of the barons of your empire.
Your liege-man I shall become
Henceforth all the days of my life,

p.25

On condition that you be my helper
So that I do not lose at all

You I shall acknowledge as sire and lord,
In the presence of your barons and earls.'
Then the king promised him,
The powerful king of England,
That willingly would he help him

As soon as he should be able.
King Henry said, in the first place,
That he should set about returning home.
He crossed the sea to England,

And went to stay at Bristol.

Then King Henry sent word
By letter and by messenger
To Robert Harding, as he held him dear,
That he should provide for the king whatever he might need,
For him and for all his men,

In every respect according to his wish.
Honourably he executed for him
All his commands.
At Bristol the king abode
A fortnight or a month, I know not which.

Whatever the king would order
Robert supplied to him in plenty.
But the king of England
For Dermot, according to the lay,
Did nothing in truth

Beyond the promise, as people say.
When King Dermot saw
That he could get no aid
From King Henry as he had promised him,
He would not stay there any longer.

King Dermot then, you must know,
Goes everywhere seeking aid:
Aid everywhere he seeks
In Wales and in England.
So far did he ask for aid

Up and down in this kingdom
That he had an interview,
So says the geste, with Earl Richard.
He was a brave earl,

Courteous, generous, and lavish.

Very earnestly the king.
Besought him, very courteously,
To give him some succour,
Or that he himself should come
To conquer his kingdom,

From which he had been wrongfully cast out.
To the earl he told plainly
How he had been betrayed by his people:
How his people had betrayed him
And driven him out and put him to flight.

His daughter he offered him to wife,
The thing in the world that he most loved:
That he would let him lave her to wife,
And would give Leinster to him,
On condition that he would aid him

So that he should he able to subdue it.
The earl at this time was a bachelor,
He had neither spouse nor wife.
When he hears from King Dermot
That he was willing to give him his daughter

On condition that he would come with him
And subdue his land for him,
The earl replies before his men:—
'Rich king, hearken unto me.
Here I assure you loyally

That I shall assuredly come to you;
But I should wish in these matters
To crave licence of the English king,
For he is the lord

Of my landed estate;

Wherefore I cannot go from his territory
Without obtaining licence in this way.'
The king assured the earl
That lie would give him his daughter
When he should come to his aid

To Ireland with his barons.
When they had concluded this accord,
The king turned straight towards Wales,
And never ceased journeying there
Until he came to St. Davids.

There the king abode
Two or three days, I know not which,
In order to equip his ships,
for he wished to cross over to Ireland.
But before King Dermot

Crossed over the salt sea,
He spake to a king in Wales
Who was very brave and courteous.
This man was called Rhys,
And was acknowledged King of Wales.

At this time King Rhys
Had a knight of great renown.
The king kept him in prison,
Robert the son of Stephen was his name.
In his prison he was keeping him,

He wished him to submit.
I know not how the king took him.
In a castle in his country.
Concerning him I will not here relate

How he was taken nor in what way;

But the rich King Dermot
Then besought King Rhys
As much as he could on behalf of the knight
That he might be able to depart freely.
Not to tell you an untruth

I know not if he was liberated then:
At the request of the rich king,
If he was liberated at that time;
But afterwards the knight
To Ireland came to aid the king.

Then King Dermot returns.
To St. Davids as soon as he could.
To Ireland then he crossed
With as many men as he had.
But Dermot, the noble king,

Did not bring with his warriors.
Any Englishmen on this occasion,
According to the account of my informant,
Except one Richard, as I have heard say,
A knight of Pembrokeshire,

Richard the son of Godibert,
A knight he was of good parts,
Together with knights, archers and serjeants,
But I know not up to what number.
For they were not long

In Ireland, these men;
For they were hardly able to do any good there
To the king in the land,

Because they were only a few men
Who crossed over in haste.

King Dermot then sent word
By letter and by messenger,
He sent over Morice Regan,
His own interpreter.
To Wales this man crossed over—

The letters of King Dermot
Which the king sent in all directions.
To earls, barons, knights,
Squires, serjeants, common soldiers,
Horse-men and foot,

In all directions the king sent word:—
'Whoever shall wish for land or pence,
Horses, armour, or chargers,
Gold and silver, I shall give them
Very ample pay;

Whoever shall wish for soil or sod
Richly shall I enfeoff them.'
He would also give them sufficient
Farm-stock and a handsome fief.
When the letters were read,

And the people understood them,
Then Robert the son of Stephen
Got himself ready the first;
He wished to cross over to Ireland
In order to aid King Dermot.

Brave knights of great renown
He brought with him, nine or ten.
One was Meiler the son of Henry,

Who was very powerful;
And Miles came there also

The son of the bishop of St. Davids.
Knights came there and barons
Whose names for the most part I do not know.
There crossed over a baron
With seven companions,

Maurice de Prendergast was his name,
As the song tells us.
Hervey too, in truth, crossed over,
He was of Mount-Maurice.
About three hundred crossed over

Knights and common folk besides.
At Bannow they landed
With all their men.
When they had landed
And had all disembarked,

They made their men encamp
On the sea-shore.
The English folk sent word
To King Dermot by messenger
That at Bannow with three ships

They had at that time landed,
And that the king should speedily
Come there without delay.
King Dermot by the direct road
Towards Bannow, next morning,

Set out very joyfully
To see the English folk.
When the king had come

To Bannow to his liegemen,
One by one he kissed them

And courteously saluted them.
That night they tarried
On the shore where they were;
But the king on the morrow
Towards Wexford directly

Went immediately, i'faith,
To attack the town.
In full force he attacked the city.
The enemy in order to protect themselves
Defended themselves from without.

At this attack the rich king
Lost eighteen of his English;
While the traitors at this time
Lost of their men only three.
All day while it was light

The attack thus lasted
Until it became late
And the men departed.
The men of Dermot the renowned
To their tents returned.

But next day, the first thing,
To King Dermot by messenger
The traitors announced
That they would give him hostages,
Would do him homage and fealty

In the presence of his baronage,
That with him they would be night and day
As with their lawful lord.

The king graciously accepted
This offer in the presence of his men.

By the advice of his English,
The noble king accepted the offer.
Thence King Dermot set out
Towards Ferns, as soon as he could,
In order to heal his wounded

And to rest his barons.
Three weeks King Dermot
Abode in the city:
Three weeks he abode
Close by the city of Ferns.

Then the king summoned
Robert and Maurice, first of all,
To come at once to confer with him
Speedily, without delay.
When the barons were come

And Dermot had greeted them
And brought them to the council,
He related all to them
How the Irish of Ossory
Greatly dreaded the English:

'Lords Barons,' so said the king,
'The Irish greatly dread you;
Wherefore, brave Knights,
With your advice in the first place,
I wish to go to Ossory

To defeat my enemies.'
The barons replied to him
That never would they be left behind,

Nor would they in any way leave
The traitors nor cease to seek for them

Until they had found them
And defeated them in open field.
Before the host advanced,
Three thousand fighting men
Made peace with King Dermot

Through dread of the English.
When the barons saw this
That so many men followed theirs,
Against the king of Ossory
They marched with the assembled host.

Consider it not, my lords, as trivial:
Bear with me a little while I tell you
How the king of Leinster
With the men whom he had so bold
Wished to enter the country

Where all his enemies were.
His enemies are in front,
Full five thousand fighting men,
Whom the king of Ossory
Had in his company.

Mac Donnchadh, the traitor,
Who was lord of Ossory,
Had thrown up before him
Three trenches wide and deep:
Before hint, within a pass,

Three trenches rapidly
Had the rebel thrown up

And erected a stockade on top.
There he offered battle
To King Dermot, without fail, that day.

There the fight took place
From morning until eventide
Between the rebel king of Ossory
And the English with great animosity.
But the English in the end

By force and by energy
Hurled the traitors thence,
By force and by strength.
But many men were wounded there,
Both killed and disabled,

Ere the stockade was won
Or forcibly wrested from them.
When King Dermot saw this
That by the might of the English
The pass was won in this way

With his men of Leinster,
He was full of confidence.
The rich King Dermot at that time
Wasted the land with fire
In order to destroy the rebel;

He sought for spoil everywhere
Up and down throughout the territory;
As much as he could find
Of the spoil he brought away with him.
Then the king marched in a different way

In order to seek the rebel Mac Donnchadh
Than he did at that time

When he put on the cope,
When he wished to parley and advise
With the rebel O'Brien, the evil one.

When the noble King Dermot
Wished to return to his own country,
Then the king called
The three renowned barons:
Robert he called by name

And Maurice, the baron,
And Hervey de Mont-Maurice
He caused also to be called.
These were at that time
Chieftains of the English.

'Lords,' quoth he, 'listen to me
For the love of God and hearken:
Draw up your men in ranks,
For well you know how to advise them.'
The barons thereupon carried out

For the king all his command:
Speedily they carried out
All the king's command.
All the men of Hy Kinsellagh
They entrusted to Donnell Kavanagh.

He was son of the King
Of Leinster, as I trow.
Whoever would wish to know the truth,
He was the foremost in the van;
While King Dermot himself

Remained with the English;
For in them King Dermot

Trusted absolutely.
Well armed were they, without doubt,
And well skilled in battle.

Now Donnell Kavanagh, in the first place,
Was about to cross through a pass
Where Dermot had formerly been
On three occasions defeated.
Wherefore the Irish dreaded

Lest they should be for the fourth time
Discomfited and defeated.
They therefore turned to flight,
So that with Donnell, the king's son,

There remained but forty-three.
Mac Donnchadh of Ossory
Soon rallies towards him his men:
He rallies his men speedily
To discomfit the Englishmen.
Know, Lords Barons,

That the English at this time
Had descended into a valley,
Both horse and foot soldiers.
For it happened that they were obliged
To pass through the middle of this valley.

Wherefore the English dreaded
The Irishmen at this time
Lest they should rush upon them
Without delay, at this moment.
For the English, as I hear,

Were hardly more than three hundred
At that time with the king,

And of the Irish, forty-three;
While their opponents, of a truth,
Were one thousand seven hundred.

Wherefore it is not to be wondered at
If the brave knights
Dreaded these people
Who were swift as the wind.
Then spake a baron:—

Maurice de Prendergast was his name—
'Lords Barons all,
Let us pass through this valley promptly
So that we may be on the mountain
On the hard field, and on the open ground.

For most of us are well armed,
Bold vassals and combatants,
While the traitors are quite naked,
They wear neither hauberks nor breast-plates;
Wherefore if we turn to hard ground

They shall have no protection from death.
We shall strike manfully,
And each together
And all united shall strike,
Footmen and horse,

Against the men of Ossory
Who will be opposed to us.
Because if they are overthrown
We shall be for ever dreaded,
And because there is no escaping

Either life or death here.'
This was the first pitched battle

That was fought, without doubt,
Between the English barons
And the Irish of Ossory.

And the Irish with great impetuosity
Followed the Englishmen.
Then Maurice exclaimed:—
'Robert Smith, come forward.
I shall tell you what to do, friend:

You shall have fifty archers;
In this thicket, of a truth,
You shall make an ambuscade for them,
Until you shall be passed.
The Irish who are behind,

When these men shall have passed,
If they dash on boldly,
You shall make an attack on them behind,
And we shall come to your aid.'
And Robert replies to the baron:—

'Sire, with the blessing of God!'
Then they went into ambush,
The forty men well armed.
 Lo! with great animosity
All the pride of Ossory

Came pursuing them
And eager for the battle.
So much did these men exert themselves
That they passed the ambuscade
Where the forty veterans

Were concealed in the thicket.

When the former had passed
By estimation they were two thousand,
And the forty archers
Did not dare to show themselves;

Because they were so few men
They lay hid without stirring.
Then had Dermot, the rich king,
Great fear for the English
Lest they should be overthrown

And brought to shame by the Irish.
And the rich King Dermot
Called Maurice to him,
Very courteouslyhe besought him
To take care of these men:

To take care of his friends
Who were left behind.
Then the baron replied:—
'Sire, at your command.
Willingly shall I aid them

And direct all my efforts thereto.'
Maurice turns aside here
Draws the rein of Blanchard;
And the Irish of Ossory
Followed the English men

Until they came into the plain,
To the hard open country.
Then they drew up their men in ranks
And very skilfully marshalled them.
Then Maurice shouted

And invoked Saint David.
The son of Stephen turned,
And Meiler, the renowned,
And Miles the son of David,
And Hervey de Mont Maurice,

And the barons, knights,
Squires, serjeants, and youths,
Against the Irish turned
And invoked St David.
And the traitors on their knees

Awaited the barons
Thus in such a way
That there was not at that time
A lance-length of ground
Between Dermot and the Irish.

When the English by their valour
Had grappled with the enemy
The Irish went away discomfited
On that day from bad to worse.
As I heard it, the truth can be told.

One of the best was Meiler;
In the battle that day
There was none better than he.
When the Irish saw this
Whom King Dermot brought

And who had earlier in the day
Fled in fear to the woods,
They returned speedily
To their lord, these men:
They joined in the combat

At the command of their lord.
You must not regard it as folly:
Eleven score of heads that day
Were brought to the king in the night,
On the Barrow where he lay,

Of his mortal enemies
Who were slain on the battle-field,
Besides the killed and wounded
Who were borne away from the field.
When these were discomfited

On the field they were left.
To Dermot, the rich king,
And to the English knights
Then spake a baron,
Robert the son of Stephen was his name:—

'Hearken unto me, valiant king,
What I counsel with the will of God:
That to-night you remain in this place,
Since God has given you the grace
That you have, Sire, by the grace of God,

Discomfited your enemies.
As soon as day shall appear
We shall go to seek the traitor,
Nor shall I ever stop before
That we go pursuing him.'

The king replies plainly
That this is not at all his pleasure:
'Rather we shall go to Leighlin
At our ease along the direct road;
Thus we shall carry our wounded

Who lie hurt on the battle-field.'
He turned to the city
Which was called Leighlin.
There they tarried for the night
To their great joy and pleasure:

By the Barrow they tarried
And lodged for the night.
On the morrow the rich king
Departed with his liege-men:
Towards Ferns they turned;

With them they carry their wounded.
When they came to the city,
Then they severally went their ways.
To their hostels to lodge
The knights returned.

They sent everywhere for physicians
To heal the sick:
To heal their wounded
They sent everywhere for physicians.
While the noble King Dermot

Abode in the city,
From all the country round about
His enemies cane to him
To crave mercy of the king
For having before completely betrayed him.

And through the dread they had
Of the English who were with him
They gave many hostages
To King Dermot, who was so bold.
And very many made peace

Through dread of the English.
The greater part of Leinster
Made peace in this manner,
Mac Donnchadh did not come in,
Who was king of Ossory;

Nor the traitor Mac Kelan,
Who was king of Offelan;
Nor Mac Torkil the traitor,
Who was lord of Dublin;
For they were in such dread of the king

That they did not dare to make peace.
Then the king speedily
Summoned his men front all sides;
Against Mac Kelan he wished to go
To shame and disgrace him.

Then the king summoned
The three noble barons
To come at once to speak to him,
Speedily, without delay.
Robert Maurice and Hervey

Promptly came to him.
The king then told them
And by word of mouth described to them
That he would go to Offelan
Against the traitor Mac Kelan,

And that they should equip themselves
To guard the person of the king.
They replied courteously:
'Sire, at your command.'
When they were ready

And had drawn up their men in ranks,
As King Dermot himself was unwilling
To separate from the English,
Donnell Kavanagh in close array
Led the van.

So much did they exert themselves
That they entered Offelan,
Plundered the whole country,
And defeated Mac Kelan;
The spoil they carried off,

And conquered and harried the people.
To Ferns then they turned
In pride and power:
Towards Ferns the king turned
With great pride and pomp.

At Ferns the noble king
Stayed for eight whole days,
And the brave English barons
Were all the time with the king.
When the eighth day was passed

Then the king summoned
His men throughout Hy Kinsellagh;
He wished to march to Glendalough,
He would plunder O'Toole
For having disdained to parley with him.

When the host was assembled,
Towards Glendalough they marched;
And the king commanded
Barons, knights and followers
That all should be ready

And equipped for battle.
Then they exclaimed:
'Noble king, march forward!
Avenge yourself, puissant king,
On your mortal enemies.

Noble king, march forward!
You shall be well avenged;
For never shall we fail you
So long as we shall live.'
Then King Dermot marches

Towards Glendalough as fast as he could.
When the king had come
With his friends and comrades,
Then he had the spoil taken
Without receiving or giving a blow.

He set about returning home,
Safe and sound, without hindrance;
And the English also
Returned quite safely.
The king returned home

With his men full of joy,
To Ferns came the barons
With all their companions.
At Ferns the king abode
As long as he pleased at that time.

His men he summoned from all sides
To come to Ferns to parley with him:
Rich and poor, in the same way,
All to come together.
The men of Wexford came

At the king's command.
At Ferns was the host assembled
With arms furnished and prepared.
Then the king summoned
Robert and Maurice, first of all,

Hervey and the baron Meiler,
And all the other knights.
The king took them into counsel:
'Hear, Sir knights,
Wherefore I summoned you here.

To Ossory I wish to go
To confound the rebel
Who has already done me high treason,
To protect my land from the traitor
That lie may never reign over *it*,

If I can*not* avenge myself on him
I shall have nothing but grief.'
Then the barons said to him:
'Sire, with God's blessing!'
Then the king summoned

Donnell Kavanagh, first of all—
That he should place himself at the head in the van
With five thousand fighting men,
And then immediately afterwards
These men of Wexford;
While the rich king himself

Remained with his English.
Through the midst of the land in this order
Marched the king of Leinster.
Into Forth he came

And descended to a river.
That night they took their hostels
Upon Mac Burtin up and down.
The men of Wexford, you must know,
Wrongfully hated the king.

Owing to their own treachery
Which they did of yore to their lord,
The traitors dreaded
The noble king night and day;
Wherefore they lodged by themselves

And night and day dreaded the king.
In this way the noble king,
Who was so gallant and courageous,
Lay by the river of Mac Burtin,
And all his host was there too.

A Phantasm came upon them in the night,
Which each one took for true.
A vast and marvellous host
Through the midst of the huts suddenly
Came upon then, well armed

With hauberks and with banded bucklers.
Those in the huts then sallied forth
To defend themselves.
A knight of the English host,
Randolf Fitz Ralph I heard hint named—

That night to keep armed watch
Randolf the barn stood outside.
The knight began greatly
To wonder at this host;
They thought that they were betrayed

By their mortal enemies.
This man shouted loud and clear:—
'St. David! Barons, Knights!'
Then he drew his brand of steel.
First of all, one of his companions,

By a blow on the helmet,
By force, he brought him to his knees;
For he thought quite certainly
That he belonged to the other side.
Most of them thought

That they were the traitors
Of the city of Wexford,
Who were *really* far off.
This phantasm then departed,
As I tell you;

It passed by the camp
To the men of Wexford.
These thought that they were being entrapped
By Dermot, the noble king.
But on the morrow they speedily

Drew up their men in ranks,
By the rich king's command,
As they were the day before.
Against the king of Ossory
Went the king with great eagerness.

Mac Donnchadh quietly
Summoned all his men
To the pass of Achadh-ur
To come without gainsaying.
A trench he then bade them throw up

High and wide, steep and deep;
And then at the back strengthen it with stakes,
And in front with hurdles,
In order to dispute the passage
With King Dermot of the bold heart.

The king marched night and day
Until he came near to Achadh-ur.
By a river of great vehemence
The warriors encamped,
And the English of great worth

Encamped round about.
On the morrow they crossed the river
Without a battle and without a contest:
On the morrow they cross, beyond a doubt,
Without a contest and without a battle.

These men of Wexford
Commenced the attack:
They began to attack the stockade.
For three whole days, i' faith,
Somewhat half-heartedly these men

Attacked the traitors.
The stockade could not be carried
By their attack in any way,
Until the English men
On the third day, as I hear,

Carried the stockade against them
And put these men to flight.
They fled as far as Tubbrid
Through the midst of the territory of Wenenath,
And from thence as far as 'Bertun'

Fled the rebel king.
But Dermot, the puissant king,
Went so far following the traitor—
So far did he pursue the traitor
That he sent him on this wandering,

Since he could not make a stand
Against King Dermot.
Then Dermot, the renowned king,
Laid waste the rebel's land,
And carried off a great spoil with him

To the city of Ferns.
Dermot, the potent king,
Had subdued his country,
Had defeated and discomfited
Most of his enemies;

Through the English he was exalted
With great pride and haughtiness.
By the advice of his people
He wished to retain, as I hear,
The soldiers of Maurice, the baron,

According to the geste that we are reading.
This man departed from King Dermot;
Full two hundred he brought away with him:
Of the English, in truth,
Maurice brought away full two hundred.

Towards Wexford he set out,
He wished to cross the sea to Wales.
Then the king sent word
To Wexford by messenger:
All the master mariners

He made obstruct Maurice
So that he could not cross the sea
Nor return to his own country.
When Maurice learnt the news,
He was in great trouble.

He feared at this time
That the traitors of Wexford
Would fall upon him
By the counsel of the king, wrongfully.
But Maurice speedily

So parleyed with these men
Of Wexford city
That they turned against the king.
Maurice did not delay at all:
He sent word to the king of Ossory

That he would come to him, without deceit,
To serve him, if he wished it;
For he had parted on bad terms
From King Dermot whom he had served.
When MacDonnchadh heard

That Maurice would come to him,
He was rejoiced at the news
And leaped to his feet with joy.
To the baron he straightway sent word
That he should certainly come to him;

Pay he would give him
Very rich and ample.
Then the baron departed,
He and all his companions;
Towards the town of Timolin

They took the direct road.
But King Dermot's son,
Donnell Kavanagh, to the best of his power,
Attacked the baron on that day
With full five hundred companions.

A great conflict they had
Maurice's men on that day;
But by force and by valour
They came to Timolin.
For three days accordingly

Maurice abode there with his followers.
Often did the king of Ossory
Send a message to these men
That he would come on the third day
Without any further gainsaying.

The king came there, of a truth,
The third day without delay:
Thither came the king of Ossory,
Mac Donnchadh, with his company;
And thereupon the king

Assumed a friendly manner towards Maurice.
Maurice and all his men
Saluted the king courteously.
The king and his chief men
Made oath to the English:

To the English they swore, in short,
On altar and on shrine,
That they would never betray them
As long as they should be with them.
Donnchadh accordingly brought away

Maurice and all his followers:
Into Ossory the king brought
Maurice and his company;
While Robert remained with Dermot
With as many men as he had,

And Hervey just in the same way
With his force and his men.
Mac Donnchadh day and night
Harried Dermot's territory:
With the aid of Maurice and his followers

He then laid waste the territory of the king.
There the baron received
The name of Maurice of Ossory:
Thus the Irish of this country
Always called him,

In that he had come to Ossory
And remained with the king.
About Maurice I shall here stop;
About a baron I wish to tell,
The son of Gerald: Maurice was his name.

The baron had landed:
He landed at Wexford
With a goodly force and many followers;
In order to aid King Dermot
He had landed at Wexford.

Then the baron sent word
To the king that he had landed.
Dermot heard the news,
For a long time none so good had come to him.
The king, with prick of spur,

To meet the baron
Set out straight to the harbour,
To the coast of Wexford.
When the rich king saw him,
He straightway said to him:—
'Be very welcome, baron,

Son of Gerald, Maurice by name.'
The latter then replies:—
'God bless you, valiant king!'
To Ferns they depart joyfully

The king and Maurice as well.
Now the king of Ossory
At this time had gone to Leix
Against the lord of that territory
To prevent his making war on him.

O'More was the name of the lord
Who held Leix at that day.
Mac Donnchadh with his English
Was about to harry all Leix,
When O'More, its lord,

With Mac Donnchadh fixed a day:
A day he fixed for him there,
He would give hostages of his country.
Not more than three or four days
Would be delay the king there.

He would give five or six hostages
The noblest of his territory.
The king granted this to him,
And abode there for three days.
O'More speedily sent word

To King Dermot that these men
By force and by war
Had entered into his territory,
And that he should come there promptly
To give him speedy succour.

Dermot, king of Leinster,
To Robert and to Fitz Gerald
All that O'More had announced
Told to the two barons;
And they then said to the king:—

'Speedily and without any respite
Get your men equipped.
There is reason, Sire, for no delay.'
The king then had it proclaimed aloud
That all who could bear arms

Should follow him at once.
The king then mounts horse.
The three barons likewise
Followed the king with their men,
Nor did they stop from there to Leix,

Where the king of Ossory was.
Now the king of Ossory
Lay in a flowery moor,
While King Dermot
Came against him, and the son of Gerald;

But he knew not, of a truth,
That men were coming against him.
So while the King Mac Donnchadh
And Maurice of Ossory
Lay in a moor

Which was very beautiful and extensive,
Maurice de Prendergast, at length,
Thought one morning
That O'More, the lord of Leix,
Was going to betray King Mac Donnchadh,

If he could in any way
Obtain a force out of Leinster.
Then lo! there comes a scout
To the king of Ossory;
He told him that King Dermot

With as large a force as he could
Was bringing the son of Stephen with him
And Maurice the son of Gerald,
And that full three hundred English
Had come with him to Leix,

Besides all the other men
Who came by tenure.
Then commenced to speak
Maurice de Prendergast first:—
'Let us go, lord king.

Too many Englishmen follow us,
And we have only a few men;
Wherefore let us go in close array.
If they approach us at all,
Well shall we be able to defend ourselves.'

Then the king went away
From the territory of O'More of Leix
By the advice of his friend
Maurice, of whom you have heard.
Speedily King Dermot,

To whom Leinster belongs,
Together with Robert and Maurice
Followed then these men;
But they did not come up with them;
For they had crossed the pass,

Mac Donnchadh of Ossory
And Maurice in whom he trusts.
Then Dermot, the puissant king,
To Ferns went in all haste:
To Ferns he returned;

Hostages he brought with him:
Hostages he brought at this time
From O'More the lord of Leix.
Mac Donnchadh with his company
Returned to Ossory.

Then they separated
Safe and sound in their country.
And the men of Ossory
Were much discontented
That they had to hire soldiers

And to give their pay to the English.
The traitors accordingly began to plot,
One behind, another in front;
They resolve to betray Maurice
And to part his treasure among them:

For their gold and silver
They resolved to murder these men.
Thus they had plotted
Treachery all in secret.
Accordingly they came before the king,

Young and old, bald and hairy:
'Hear us, king, good lord!
Maurice we wish, at length, to put to death;
We have a sufficiently good peace;
Of them we have no further need.'

And the king replied:—
'Please God and his might
That they may never be betrayed by me,
Murdered, killed, disgraced, or taken!'
To the king came the baron,

Knowing nothing of the treachery
Then indeed he demanded
Of the king free licence
That he might return home to his country.
The king, be sure, with much regret

Gave leave to the knight
To return to his country;
But the king besought him much
To remain with him still.
Maurice replied to the king:—

'The English wish to cross over:
They wish to cross the high sea
To visit their friends.'
Then the king departed,
According to the geste which you now hear;

To Fertakerach he went, I think,
While the English at Kilkenny
Remained that night
With great joy and in great commotion;
While all the wicked traitors

Of that territory round about
Went to plash the passes
Through which they had to pass.
But as God willed it
That Maurice should be forewarned

Of the great crime
That these men of Ossory did,
The baron caused to be summoned
All his companions to him.
When they were assembled,
And Maurice told them
How the men of Ossory
By their great treachery
Had contrived an ambuscade for them
With two thousand men well armed:

How the Irish are in front of them
With two thousand fighting men
'In a strong place in order to obstruct us
That we cannot pass that way.
Take counsel, Sir barons,

Concerning this affair how we shall act.'
They all replied:—
'Let the counsel rest with you.'
To their hostels they returned
Where they were before lodged.

Very quietly they kept themselves,
As though they knew nothing about it.
Then Maurice of Ossory
To the Seneschal of Mac Donnchadh—
To the Seneschal sent word

That for half a year or a quarter
He was willing to remain with the king,
As they had previously been.
Speedily the king sent word
That he would come to parley with the English.

When was spread and published
The news throughout the country,
That Maurice had remained
With the king of that country,
The traitors returned home

From the pass where they were in ambush.
In the night when they were asleep
Maurice then sent word
By a private page
That all the barons should take horse,

Archers, squires, and sergeants,
Both small and great.
Those who wished to cross over
Soon equipped themselves:
They got themselves ready

Nor would they delay any longer.
Towards the sea they turned
To cross to their own countries.
To the city of Waterford,
As fate led them,

The knights came
Safe and sound and none missing.
There the barons stayed
With all their companions.
But there they were hindered

Through a man who was wounded:—
For a foot-soldier
Had wounded a citizen,
Who afterwards died of the wound.
Nor did they consider it as sport

The citizens of the city
Of Waterford, as I have mentioned.
There they were arrested
All the illustrious barons;
But by the counsel of their lord

Maurice, who was their pleader,
And by his good sense and tact,
Maurice enabled them all to cross over.
In Wales they all landed
Safe and sound, joyous and glad.

About these men we shall here leave off,
About King Dermot we shall tell you.
I wish to tell of King Dermot
How he delivered Wexford
To a noble baron,

The son of Stephen, Robert the baron.
And Maurice the son of Gerald
Fortified himself at Carrick,
By the permission and by the desire
Of Dermot, the potent king.

Then soon afterwards
Earl Richard sent over
Some of his men to Ireland,
With nine or ten of his barons.
The first was Raymond le Gros,

A bold and daring knight.
At Dundonuil they landed
Where they then constructed a fort
By the permission of the rich king
Dermot, who was so courteous.

There Raymond le Gros remained
With his knights and barons.
Then he plundered the territory,
Took and killed the cows.
But the men of Waterford

And of Ossory likewise
Assembled their hosts;
Against Dundonuil they resolved to go
In order to attack the fort.
They think surely to shame the English.

Donnell O'Phelan of the Decies,
And O'Ryan of Odrone,
And all the Irish of the country
Surrounded the fort.
By estimation the Irish were

As many as three or four thousand;
Raymond and his men
Were not more than a hundred.
They drove the cows into the fort
By the counsel of Raymond.

The men of Waterford
Came very fiercely
To demolish the fort;
They think to disgrace the English.
Raymond speaks to his men:—

'Sir barons, hearken to me.
You see your enemies coming
Who have resolved to attack you.
It is more honourable for you here
Than within to be killed or taken.

Come now, do you all arm yourselves,
Knights, sergeants, and archers;
Thus shall we place ourselves in open field
In the name of the Almighty Father.'
The knights and the barons,

By the advice of Raymond le Gros,
Resolved to sally from the gates
In order to charge the Irish.
The cows were scared
At the men who were armed;

And owing to the tumult that they made
The cows all in front
By force and by strength
Sallied forth at the gate.
This was the first company

That sallied from the fort, I trow.
Upon the Irish they rushed
In a short space, in a few moments.
The Irish could not stand against them:
They were forced to separate;

And Raymond with his English
Threw himself amid the Irish.
Wherefore they were divided,
The Irish were discomfited,
So that the last company

Fled away through this fright.
There they were discomfited
All the Irish of this district.
On the field a thousand were left
Vanquished, killed, wounded, or taken.

By the force and by the strength
That the good Jesus created against them
And through dread and through fear
They were enfeebled that day.
Of the Irish there were taken

Quite as many as seventy.
But the noble knights
Had them beheaded.
To a wench they gave
An axe of tempered steel,

And she beheaded them all
And then threw their bodies over the cliff,
Because she had that day
Lost her lover in the combat.

Alice of Abervenny was her name
Who served the Irish thus.
In order to disgrace the Irish
The knights did this.
And the Irish of the district

Were discomfited in this way.
To their country they returned
Outdone and discomfited:
To their country they returned
Discomfited and outdone.
At Dundonuil remained Raymond

He and all his companions,
And Hervey de Mont Maurice
And Walter Bluet likewise.
They kept very much to themselves,
As against these Irishmen.

According to the statement of the old people,
Very soon afterwards Earl Richard
Landed at Waterford.
Full fifteen hundred men he brought with him.
On the eve of St. Bartholomew

Did the earl land.
The most powerful persons in the city
Were called Ragnald and Sidroc.
On St. Bartholomew's day,
Earl Richard, the prudent,

Took by assault and won
The city of Waterford.
But there were many killed there
Of the citizens of Waterford
Before that it was won

Or taken by assault against them.
When the earl by his power
Had taken the city,
The earl immediately sent word
To King Dermot by messenger

That he had come to Waterford
And had won the city,
That the rich king should come to him
And should bring his English.
King Dermot speedily

Came there, be sure, right royally.
The king in his company
Brought there many of his barons,
And his daughter he brought there;
To the noble earl he gave her.

The earl honourably
Wedded her in the presence of the people.
King Dermot then gave
To the earl, who was so renowned—
Leinster he gave to him

With his daughter, whom he so much loved,
Provided only that he should have the lordship
Of Leinster during his life.
And the earl granted
To the king all his desire.

Then they turned aside
The king and Earl Richard.
Raymond le Gros joined them.
A bold and daring knight,
And Maurice de Prendergast

Likewise, as I hear;
For with the earl, of a truth,
He had returned, as people say.
By the advice of the earl
The warrior had returned.

At this council in sooth
Was Meiler the son of Henry,
And many a brave knight
Whose names I cannot mention.
There all the brave knights

Proceeded to advise
That they should go straight to Dublin
And should assault the city.
Then the king departed
Towards Ferns with his English.

He caused his men to be summoned
Everywhere and in great force.
When they were all assembled,
Towards Waterford they set out directly.
Earl Richard then gave

The city in charge of his men:
In Waterford he then left
A portion of his followers.
Then they turned towards Dublin
The king and the renowned earl.

Now all the pride of Ireland
Was at Clondalkin in a moor,
And the king of Connaught
Was at Clondalkin at this time.
In order to attack the English

He divided his troops.
They plashed the passes everywhere
In order to obstruct the English,
So that in fact they should not come
To Dublin without hostility.

And king Dermot was warned
By a scout whom he had sent
That the Irish were in front
About 30,000 strong.
King Dermot sent to ask

The earl to come to parley with him.
The earl speedily
Came promptly to the king.
'Sir Earl,' thus spake the king,
'Hearken to me at this time:

Draw up your men in ranks
And marshal your sergeants.
We shall now go by the mountain
On the hard field and on the open ground;
For the woods are plashed

And the roads trenched across,
And all our enemies of Ireland
Are before us in a moor.'
The earl then summoned
All the brave knights.

Miles came to him, first of all,
A noble and brave warrior:
Miles had the name de Cogan
And his body was bold and burly.
He was at the head in front

With seven hundred English soldiers;
And Donnell Kavanagh likewise
Remained with these men.
And then afterwards Raymond le Gros
With about eight hundred companions.

In the third company the rich king
With about a thousand Irish.
And Richard, the courteous earl,
Had with him three thousand English.
In this company there were about

Four thousand vassals, I trow.
In the rear-guard the king
Had the Irish drawn up in ranks.
They were all well armed,
The renowned English barons.

By the mountain did the king
Guide the English host that day.
Without a battle and without a contest
They arrived at the city.
Moreover the city was that day

Taken beyond gainsaying:
The day of St. Matthew the Apostle
The city of Dublin was burning.
When the Irish saw this
That King Dermot was come

And the earl also
With all his English troops,
And that the illustrious liege barons
Had surrounded the city,
The king of Connaught went away

Without a word at this time,
And the Irish from this district
To their country departed.
Hasculf MacTorkil, the deceiver,
Remained in the city that day,

In order to defend the city
Of which he was acknowledged
Sire, lord, and defender,
Through all the country.
Outside the walls of the city

Was the king encamped;
While Richard, the good earl,
Who was lord of the English,
Remained with his English
And with King Dermot himself.

Nearest to the city
Was Miles encamped,
The good Miles de Cogan
Who was afterwards lord of Mount Brandon,
Which is the wildest spot,

Mountain or plain, in the world.
Now Dermot, the noble king,
Despatched Morice Regan,
And by Morice proclaimed
To the citizens of the city

That without delay, without any respite,
They should surrender without gainsaying:
Without any further gainsaying
They should surrender themselves to their lord.
Thirty hostages demanded

King Dermot of the city.
But those within, i'faith,
Could not separate among themselves
The hostages of the city
Who should be delivered to the king.

Hasculf accordingly made answer
To Dermot, the renowned king,
That on the morrow speedily
He would perform all his command.
It greatly vexed the baron,

The good Miles de Cogan,
That the parley lasted so long
Between the king and all his people.
Miles shouted all at once
'Barons, knights, A Cogan!'

Without the king's command
And without the earl's either,
He attacked the city.
The baron Miles with his followers
With audacity and with great fury

Then set upon the city.
The baron Miles, the renowned,
By main force took the city.
Before that Dermot knew it that day
Or Richard the good earl,

Had Miles, the strong-limbed baron,
Actually entered into Dublin,
Had already conquered the city,
And put MacTorkil to flight.
And the men of Dublin

Fled away by the sea;
But many remained there
Who were killed in the city.
Much renown acquired that day
Miles who was of such worth;

And the renowned barons
Found much wealth:
In the city they found
Much treasure and other wealth.
Thereupon there came

The king and the earl riding quickly:
To the city they came
The king and the earl together.
And Miles, the renowned baron,
To the earl gave up the city:

The city Miles gave up,
And the earl thereupon received it.
Much provision they found
And good victuals in great plenty.
The earl then abode

While he pleased in the city;
And the king returned
To Ferns in his own country.
But on the festival of St. Remy,
When August was over,

Soon after Michaelmas,
Richard, the noble earl,
To Miles delivered, you must know,
The wardship of the city.
To Waterford he set out

The earl and his ample suite.
There the earl abode
So long as it pleased him.
At Ferns then tarried
King Dermot during this winter.

The king, who was so noble,
Lies buried at Ferns.
All the Irish of the country

Revolted against the earl.
Of the Irish at this time

There remained with him only three:
Donnell Kavanagh, in the first place,
Who was brother to his wife,

O'Reilly of Tirbrun,
And thirdly Auliffe O'Garvy;
While the Irish of Hy Kinsellagh,
Who were with King Murtough,
They then stirred up a great war

Against the earl of Leinster.
And the rich king of Connaught
Summoned to him
The Irish of all Ireland
In order to lay siege to Dublin.

They came on the day
That their lord had appointed for them.
When they were assembled
They were sixty thousand strong.
At Castleknock, at this time,

Was the rich king of Connaught;
And MacDunlevy of Ulster
Planted his standard at Clontarf;
And O'Brien of Munster
Was at Kilmainham with his brave men;

And Murtough, as I hear,
Was near Dalkey with his men.
The earl, you must know, at this time
Was within the city, of a truth.
The son of Stephen promptly sent

Some of his men to the earl:
In order to aid and succour him
He sent men to him at this crisis.
When Robert had sent
About thirty-six of his men

To aid the earl Richard,
Who was *the subject of such anxiety,*
The traitors without any delay
Fell upon Robert.
In the town of Wexford

They wrongfully slew his men:
His men they utterly betrayed,
Killed, cut to pieces, and brought to shame.
Within a castle on the Slaney,
According to what the geste here tells,

The traitors took Robert
And put him in prison at Begerin:
Five knights, in short,
They imprisoned in Begerin.
And there came Donnell Kavanagh

And the Irish of Hy Kinsellagh:
To Dublin he came
To the noble earl at this juncture.
With him came O'Reilly,
And Auliffe also.

To the earl they told all,
How Robert was imprisoned,
And how his men were slain,
Discomfited, and treacherously killed.
The earl thereupon replies:—

'Donnell, let it not appear,
Let it not appear, my friend,
That our men are brought to shame.'
The earl then summoned
The the lord councillors

To come to him at once to advise
Speedily, without delaying.
There came Robert de Quency,
And Walter de Riddlesford came,
A brave and noble warrior;

Maurice de Prendergast also
Came, as I hear;
And there came the good Miles,
Under heaven there was no better baron;
And Meiler the son of Henry,

And Miles the son of David,
And Richard de Marreis came there,
Noble and courteous knights;
And Walter Bluet came there;
Knights barons as many as twenty:

All the barons of great worth
Came to their lord.
When the renowned barons
Were assembled in council,
The earl sought counsel

Of all his kinsfolk and friends.
'My lords,' thus spake the valiant earl,
'May God of Heaven protect us!
You see, my lords, your enemies
Who have now besieged you here.

We shall have hardly anything to eat
Before the fortnight is out:
(For the measure of corn
Was sold for a silver mark,
And for a measure of barley

One got at that time half a mark:)
Wherefore, Sir Knights,
Let us send a message to the king.'
Then the renowned earl
Sent a message to the king

That he would become his man
And would hold Leinster of him.
'Come now, free-born lords,
To the king of Connaught two vassals
By your counsel we shall despatch,

And we shall send the archbishop,
That I shall be willing to do fealty to him,
And will hold Leinster of him.'
An archbishop they sent,
Who was afterwards called St. Laurence.

The archbishop they then sent
And Maurice de Prendergast with him.
To the king they accordingly announced
The message of the earl.
Thereupon the king said to them

Without taking time or respite:
He answered to the messenger
That he would by no means do this;
No more than Waterford
Dublin and Wexford alone

Would he leave to Earl Richard
Of all Ireland as his share;
Not a whit more would he give
To the earl or to his followers.
The messengers turned back

To the city of Dublin:
The messengers returned
Speedily without delaying.
Aloud they tell their message
In the hearing of all the barons:

To the earl they told completely
The reply of the haughty king:—
That he would not give him more land
In the whole of Leinster,
Except only the three cities

Which I have already named to you;
And if this did not meet his pleasure
They would attack the city;
If he would not accept this offer
The king would hear no more,

For on the morrow, so said the king,
The English would be attacked.
When the earl had heard
What the archbishop related,
Then the earl caused to be summoned

Miles de Cogan the light of limb:
'Make all your men arm, barons,
Sally forth in the foremost van;
In the name of the Almighty Father
In the foremost van sally forth.'

About forty horsemen
Are with Miles before in the front,
Sixty archers and one hundred sergeants
Had Miles under his orders.
And then next, Raymond le Gros

With forty companions,
And he had one hundred fighting-men
And three-score archers.
And then next, the good earl
With forty fighting-men

With one hundred hardy sergeants
And three-score archers.
Very well armed they were
Horsemen, sergeants, and hired soldiers.
When the earl had sallied forth

With his friends and his comrades,
Miles placed himself at the head in the van
With two hundred fighting vassals;
And then next Raymond le Gros
With about two hundred companions;

In the third company the noble earl
With two hundred hardy vassals.
Donnell Kavanagh, of a truth,
Auliffe O'Garvy likewise,
And O'Reilly of Tirbrun,

Of whom you have already heard,
Were in the van with Miles,
As the Song tells us.
But the Irish of the district
Knew nought of this affair:

Of the barons thus armed,
And equipped for battle.
Miles de Cogan very quickly
By the direct road towards Finglas
Towards their stockades thereupon

Set out at a rapid pace.
When Miles had drawn near
To where the Irish were encamped,
'A Cogan!' he shouted aloud,
'Strike, in the name of the Cross!

Strike, barons, nor delay at all,
In the name of Jesus the son of Mary!
Strike, noble knights,
At your mortal enemies!'
The renowned liege barons

At their huts and cabins
Attacked the Irish
And fell upon their tents;
And the Irish unarmed
Fled through the moors:

Throughout the country they fled away
Like scattered cattle.
Raymond le Gros also
Oft invoked St. David,
And went pursuing the Irish

To work his will upon them;
And Richard the good earl
Did so well that day,
So well did the earl do,
That all were astonished;

And Meiler the son of Henry,
Who was of such renown,
Bore himself so bravely
That men wondered.
A hundred and more were slain

While bathing where they were beset,
And more than one thousand five hundred
Of these men were slain,
While of the English there was wounded
Only one foot-sergeant.

The field remained that day
With Richard, the good earl,
And the Irish departed
Discomfited and outdone:
As God willed, at that time,

The field remained with our English.
So much provision did they find,
Corn, meal, and bacon,
That for a year in the city
They had victuals in abundance,

To the city with his men
The earl went very joyfully.
Earl Richard, light of limb,
Makes preparations for his journey.
To Wexford he resolved to go

To set free the baron.
The baron the son of Stephen
The traitors hold in prison:
The traitors of Wexford hold him, in short,
Imprisoned in Begerin.

The wardship of Dublin he gave
To the good Miles the warrior.
Then the earl proceeded
Towards Wexford night and day.
So much did the earl accomplish

By his day's marches, and so far go,
For so many nights and so many days
That he tame to Odrone.
Now the Irish of the district
Were assembled at the pass:

To meet the earl Richard
At one side they were assembled:
To attack the English
Were the Irish assembled.
The earl Richard with his men

Through the midst of the pass in safety
Thought surely to advance,
When an obstacle met him.
The rebel king of Odrone,
O'Ryan was his name,

Shouted out loudly:
'To your destruction, Englishmen, have you come!'
He rallied his men to him,
And attacked the English sharply;
And the English, of a truth,

Manfully defended themselves.
But Meiler, the son of Henry
Carried the prize that day:
In the battle, knew in sooth,
There was no better than the son of Henry.

And much renowned that day
Was Nichol, a cowled monk;
For with an arrow he slew that day
The lord of Odrone:
By an arrow, as I tell you,

Was O'Ryan slain that day.
And Meiler, the strong-limbed baron,
Was stunned by a blow
Of a stone in this fight,
So that he reeled to the ground.

But when O'Ryan was slain
The Irish separated.
This wood was afterwards named
And called the earl's pass,
Because the earl was attacked there

By his enemies.
Thence the earl turned
Towards Wexford city
To liberate the imprisoned Robert,
Of whom I have before told you.

But the perfidious traitors
Would not deliver him up to the earl.
To Begerin they fled
And Wexford they set on fire.
For the sea ran entirely

All around Begerin;
Werefore the noble earl,
Could not, i' faith, get at them.
Then the earl set out
Towards Waterford with his followers.

To the king of Limerick he sent word
By his sealed letters
That he should come to Ossory
With all his baronage
Against MacDonnchadh the king

Who held sway in Ossory.
For the king of Limerick had
A daughter of the rich king Dermot;
A daughter of Dermot on the other hand
Earl Richard had to wife;

So that they had to wife two sisters
King O'Brien and the earl.
He came in great force
Into Ossory with his men.
Earl Richard, the good earl,

Went to meet O'Brien that day
To Idough with his brave men,
To meet the king of Munster,
Where there were about two thousand men
Of the noble earl and King O'Brien.

MacDonnchadh sent a messenger
To the earl to tell him
That he would of his own accord come
To the earl, to whom he would redress
The outrage and the wrong

With which the barons had upraided him.
To the earl he would come, in short, to parley,
On condition that he could freely return,
Provided that Maurice the baron
Of Prendergast, as we tell in our song,

Should take him by the hand upon his faith.
To safe-conduct the rich king,
And Maurice at once
To the earl speedily
Went; the noble baron

Obtained from the earl peace for the king.
The earl replied to him:—
'Maurice, you do wrong to fear;
Make the king come to me;
When it shall please him he can depart.'

And Maurice, as I trow,
From each baron individually
Exacted an oath
That he might bring him securely,
And that in safety he could depart

Whenever it should please him.
And Maurice, the vassal,
Then mounted his horse,
And straightway departed
To meet the king with all speed.

To the court he then brought him
Before the earl in safety.
The earl then accused him—
As did all the renowned barons,—
MacDonnchadh of Ossory,

Of his great treachery:
In what manner he had betrayed
The good Dermot, the noble king.
King O'Brien counsels
The noble earl, the warrior,

That he should have the traitor seized
And should have him consigned to infamy;
And the barons, i'faith,
Were all willing to consent thereto.
And King O'Brien of Munster

Sent his men through the land:
Made his men go everywhere
To plunder the land,
While MacDonnchadh was
Before the earl and was pleading.

When Maurice, the baron,
Was warned of this treachery,
He sent word to his men everywhere
That they should arm themselves quickly.
Then Maurice exclaimed:

'Barons, what are you meditating?
Ye have broken your oaths,
Towards me ye are forsworn.'
To his followers Maurice said:
'To horse, illustrious cavaliers!'

Maurice by his sword sware
That there was no vassal so bold
As on the king that day
Should lay a hand to his dishonour
But, right or wrong,

Should have his head struck in two.
And Richard, the valiant earl,
To the baron Maurice thereupon
Gave up MacDonnchadh,
And delivered him by the hand.

Then the baron mounts horse,
He and all his companions;
The king they brought at length
To the woods in safety.
They met O'Brien's men

Who had spoiled the land,
And Maurice then slew
Nine or ten of these men;
And by force and by valour
From his lord's court

Did Maurice and his followers
Bring the king to the wood that day.
And Maurice de Prendergast lay
With MacDonnchadh that night,
But next day in the morning

Maurice returned
To the court of his lord
Who was of so great worth.
The barons blamed Maurice
For having brought the king to the wood,

In that he was the mortal enemy
Of Richard the good and lawful earl;
For this king by his war
Cast out Dermot from Leinster.
And Maurice folded his glove

And gave it to his lord as a pledge
That he would redress in his court
Whatever transgression he had committed.
And the renowned English vassals
Went sufficient security for him.

When they had finished this pleading
King O'Brien goes to Limerick.
The earl then set out
Straight to the city of Ferns.
Eight days he abode there,

The noble earl and his baronage.
Then the earl sent in all directions
Squires, sergeants, and attendants;
Murtough O'Brien they go to seek
Up and down throughout the land.

So well did they seek him through the country
That they found him, in truth, and took him.
Straight to the city of Ferns
They then led the rebel O'Brien
To the earl they then delivered him,

O'Brien the convicted traitor.
Because the rebel had betrayed
Dermot his rightful lord,
The earl had him beheaded
And his body then thrown to the hounds.

The dogs wholly devoured him
And ate up his flesh.
And one of his sons Donnell Kavanagh
Had taken and brought to the earl.
At Ferns they were both put to death

In the presence of the people of that district.
The Irish king of Hy Kinsellagh
Then made peace with the earl;
This was the rebel Murtough
Who was then king of Hy Kinsellagh.

The earl then granted to him
The kingdom of Hy Kinsellagh;
The pleas of Leinster he entrusted
To Donnell Kavanagh, the son of Dermot.
These two were called kings

Of the Irish of the country.
In Ireland there were several kings,
As elsewhere there were earls;
But whoever holds Meath and Leinster
And Desmond and Munster

And Connaught and Ulster,
Which the six brothers formerly held,
Those who hold these are head-kings
Of Ireland, according to the Irish.
When the earl had appeased

The Irish of the country,
Then the English king sent
To the earl to announce
That, without delay, without gainsaying,
Without taking time or respite,

The earl should come speedily
To speak to him at once.
And the earl at this juncture
To Miles gave the custody of Dublin:
A city much renowned,

Which was formerly called Ath-Cliath.
And the custody of the city of Waterford,
Which was called Port-Lairge,
The noble Earl Richard gave :
To Gilbert de Boisrohard.

The earl then got ready,
He resolved to cross over to England;
The noble earl resolved to cross over
To speak to King Henry:
To King Henry Curt-Mantel,

Who was his rightful lord,
His ships he then equipped
To traverse the waves.
He resolved to cross the high seas,
He will go to speak to the English king.

So much did the earl hasten
That he soon crossed the sea.
In Wales he landed,
The earl who was so much dreaded.
Earl Richard at this time

At Pembroke found the rich king.
The noble earl of great worth
Into the presence of his lord,
With his friends and his comrades
Into the presence of his lord came.

The noble earl saluted him
In the name of the Son of the King of Majesty
And the king graciously
Made answer to Earl Richard.
The king thereupon replied:

'May God Almighty bless you!'
Now, as it was told to me,
The earl was somewhat embroiled:
The noble earl of great worth
Was embroiled with his lord.

Through the lies of people
And through evil instigation
Was Richard, the noble earl,
Somewhat embroilled with King Henry.
Nevertheless the rich king

Towards the earl assumed a friendly manner.
The rich king at this time
Made no show of anger;
But King Henry, who was the empress' son,
Honoured him much.

Then while the warrior
Remained with his lord,
Lo! a rebel thereupon
To Dublin came sailing.
Below Dublin he landed,

Hasculf MacTorkil with a hundred ships.
He brought many men with him:
About twenty thousand he got ready.
From the Isles they came and from Man;
And from Norway came John.

A brave man, John the Wode,
MacTorkil brought with him.
He was nephew of the rich king
Of Norway, according to the Irish.
At the Steine they landed,

Hasculf and John the Wode.
Outside Dublin city
Were these men encamped.
In order to attack the city
They disembarked their men.

The good Miles armed himself,
He and all his companions.
The noble man resolved to defend himself
So long as he could have defence:
With the aid of Almighty God

He resolved to defend himself against these men.
Then behold! a king
Of this country, an Irishman,
Gilmoholmock was his name,
He was at peace with the good Miles;

With Miles he came to parley,
To ask counsel of the baron.
For Miles of the bold heart
Held hostages of this king,
That he would hold with the earl

Loyally night and day.
The good Miles said to the king:
'Hearken, Sire, a moment.
I shall deliver up your hostages to you
Safe and sound and all complete:

You shall have your hostages on condition
That you do what I tell you,
On condition that you aid
Neither us nor them at all,
But that you stand to one side of us

And watch the battle
From the side with your men,
So that you may see clearly
The contest and the battle
Between us and them, without fail.

And if God grants it to us
That these men be discomfited,
Then that you aid us with your force
To overthrow them;
And if we be recreant

That you aid their men in all things
To cut us to pieces and slay us
And hand our men over to destruction.'
The king granted this to him,
Pledged his faith and sware

That all that Miles said to him
The king would do without any delay.
Gilmoholmock thereupon
Outside the city instantly
Posted himself, in truth, the king

With the men of his district.
On the summit of the Howe over the Stein,
In a plain, outside the city,
To watch the contest
They were assembled:

To watch the combat
Gilmoholmock posted himself that day;
In an open place, of a truth,
He posted himself with his followers.
Lo! John the Wode

Towards Dublin with serrid ranks,
Towards the city with his men,
Against the eastern gate,
Towards St. Mary's gate,
They then attacked the city.

Now Miles, with the undaunted mien,
Had a brother, a brave baron.
Richard was his name,
Brother he was to good Miles.
He armed himself well,

With him about thirty horsemen.
Through the western entrance
They issued quite secretly,
So that none knew of it,
Not a single one except his brother.

And Miles marshalled his men,
He wished to defend the city,
The sergeants he made go in front
To hurl their lances and shoot their arrows.
These men close to the walls

In order to defend the battlements
Thereupon turned,
Both archers and sergeants.
And Miles, who was so daring,
With all his knights of worth

Were mounted on their horses
With arms furnished and prepared.
John's men with great fury
Then fell upon the city,
And the English of great worth

Defended themselves well that day.
And Richard came
Before that they were perceived,
Upon the guard that was behind;
Loudly he shouted.

Richard thereupon shouts:
'Strike, valiant knights!'
And the barons with great force
Threw themselves into the throng.
Very great was the contest

And the hue and cry.
And John then scented
The noise of those behind and the shouting;
From the city he departed,
He wished to succour his friends

Who were left behind,
Nine or ten thousand, I know not which.
They departed from the city,
This John and his followers,
To succour their men behind

That they should not be outdone.
And Miles, the renowned,
Made a sortie from the city:
Made a sortie with his men,
With about three hundred armed vassals

Besides all his other followers,
Archers, sergeants and foot-soldiers.
Before Miles made his sortie
Five hundred were laid low;
And these five hundred were wounded

So that they shall never be healed.
When Miles came up
And the strong-limbed English vassals,
Miles then shouted out:
'Strike, renowned barons!

Strike, vassals, speedily,
Spare not these men!'
When Miles was on the field,
He and all his companions,
Very much emboldened were

The hardy English vassals:
As God Almighty willed it,
By his power which is so great,
According to the statement of the history,
To the English he gave the victory.

But of the English on that day
Was Richard the flower of all.
A very severe punishment there was
Of these men near the sea.
Thereupon they fled,

Both small and great,
From this great hue that they had brought on,
Hasculf and John the Wode.
When Gilmoholmock, you must know, the king
Saw the Northmen take to flight,

Both those from the Isles and those from Man,
The followers of Hasculf and of John,
And the king perceived for certain
That they were discomfited,
To his feet the king leaped,

And with a loud voice shouted:
'Up now, brave sirs!
Let us aid the free-born English
Up now, quickly! we shall aid
Good Richard and Miles.'

And the Irish thereupon
Went in all directions slaying:
Slaying they went in all directions
With their javelins and their darts
These men who had come

With Hasculf, the old hoary-head.
And these went away discomfited
To the woods and moors and wastes.
Why should I say more?
Fifteen hundred to their destruction

Were left on that day,
Dead and miserably hacked.
Indeed, some people say
Two thousand brave warriors
Were, in truth, left that day

Who were previously slain on the battle-field.
Now this John the Wode
Was a very renowned warrior;
For this John in the contest
With a well-tempered axe

Struck a knight that day
Whose thigh he chopped off:
With his axe of hard iron
He chopped the thigh off to the ground.
He slew that day about

Nine or ten of our English.
But the good Miles de Cogan
Killed the aforesaid John.
And Richard that day, without fail,
Took Hasculf prisoner in the battle.

And the fields and the wastes
Were covered with the slain.
Know all for certain, without fail,
There was in the battle that day
Great destruction, in short,

And ruin at the hands of the English.
A goodly treasure the English gained
Of silver and gold;
And Miles and his followers
Returned to Dublin.

When they came to the city
They then beheaded Hasculf;
On account of his outrageous conduct
They rightfully beheaded him:
On account of his insolence and mad sayings,

After Richard had taken him prisoner,
They speedily beheaded him,
In the presence of the sea-folk.
The Northmen fled away
Over mountain and plain;

To the ships they turned their skiffs,
They fully thought to cross the sea;
But the English are behind them
To dispute their ships with them.
If you had been there on that day,

Of the men of Hasculf the traitor
You would have seen five hundred plunge
Into the depths of the sea.
Thus, of a truth, were
The sea-folk discomfited.

The English by the aid of God
Had that day won the field.
Their enemies were scattered,
Killed, wounded, and discomfited.
To their country, of a truth,

Of these Northmen
There returned only two thousand
To claim their rights.
Here we shall leave the story
Of the good Richard and of Miles;

Of the English king we shall tell you,
Of Henry with the stern aspect.
As soon as the king came to the sea
At Pembrokeshire, in order to cross over,
Lo! then at the harbour

Twelve traitors from Wexford
Came to land in a boat
At Pembroke close under the castle.
As soon as they had landed,
Towards the castle they turned;

The caitiffs wanted to speak
To king Henry Curt-Mantel.
So far did the traitors go
That they entered the palace
Into the presence of King Henry,

Who was the son of the empress,
And they saluted him aloud
In the name of God the Father Almighty.
The rich king straightway
Replied to them graciously,

That they were welcome,
His well wishers and his friends.
'Hold it not, lord, as folly,'
Thus spake the traitors unto him,
'If we shall say to you—be it known to you all—

Why we have come to you.
We have taken your rebellious vassal,
Robert Fitz Stephen is his name,
Who was guilty of perfidy towards you of yore,
Often of great evil and treachery;

Many times has he waged war against you.
In Wales and in England;
To Ireland he came with a ship,
He wished to hand us over to destruction,
He wished to destroy our country,

Often did he put us from bad to worse.
In a castle we took him,
In a strong prison we have placed him;
To thee we shall give him up, noble king,
Who art lord of the English,

And do you, noble renowned king,
Do your pleasure in this matter.'
The king replied to them:
'On this condition be ye welcome,
That you hand over this man to me

And then ye will see what I shall do with him.'
And they assured the king
And promised truly and swore
That, as soon as they had crossed the sea,
To king Henry, who was so stern,

They would at length hand over Robert
And all the other knights
As many as they had in prison
And in their possession.
Now, my lords, I will tell you

Why the king, who was so well-bred,
Showed such great wrath
Against the renowned baron Robert;
For, of a truth, the king,
To whom England belongs,

Loved the baron much
Whom these men held in prison;
Wherefore the king feared
That the perfidious traitors
Would murder the good Robert

Or bring him to shame and dishonour;
Wherefore the king made pretence
Of anger and of great wrath
That he had for the baron,
For fear of the treachery

Which these knaves might do
Against Robert, the warrior.
The king accordingly thanked
The traitors for their loyalty,
In that they had taken his enemy

And put him in gyves and fetters,
And in that they had promised him
To deliver up Robert to him.
Then the traitors took
Their leave of King Henry

And went away to their hostel
The chief one in the city.
There they waited for the wind,
The king and they in the same way.
Hear, my lords, concerning King Henry,

Who was the son of the empress,
How he resolved to cross the sea
And to conquer Ireland
Entirely through the recommendation
Of the noble earl, according to the people.

King Henry then crossed over
To Ireland with his ships.
The king then brought with him
Four hundred armed knights.
King Henry when he took ship

Put to sea at the Cross:
At Pembrokeshire at this time
The rich king put to sea.
With him the noble earl crossed over,
According to the statement of the old people.

At Waterford the noble king
Landed with four thousand English,
On All Hallows' Day, of a truth,
If the geste does not deceive us;
Before the feast of St. Martin

The king at length came to Ireland.
With the king there crossed over
Vassals of good kindred.
William the son of Audeline
Came with him on this occasion,

Also Humphrey de Bohun,
And the baron Hugh de Lacy.
With the king himself there came
The son of Bernard, Robert, I trow;
A renowned baron came,

Bertram de Verdun he was called;
Earls and barons of great worth
Came in numbers with Henry.
The earl of his own free will
Surrendered the city to the king:

To the king he surrendered Waterford
Of his own will and agreement.
Homage for Leinster
He did to the king of England:
The earl of great worth

Did homage to his lord.
The rich king granted to him
Leinster in fee.
King Henry, the gallant,
To the Baron Robert the son of Bernard—

The custody of the city of Waterford
He then gave to the son of Bernard.
When the king had landed
At Waterford in safety,
Lo! the traitors,

Who were lords of Wexford,
Brought the son of Stephen
Into his presence in chains.
In the city of Waterford
To the king himself they delivered him up.

The king received the body
In the presence of his barons and earls.
There the noble king accused him
Of whatever transgression he had done
Towards him, who was his lord,

In the presence of the traitors.
The son of Stephen folded his glove,
And straightway offered it to the king:
For whatever he should be able to accuse him of
Robert would be willing to give redress

In his court very willingly
On the guaranty of all his peers.
French, Flemmings and Normans
Went sufficient bail for him at once.
From Waterford King Henry

Set out with his marquises,
To Dublin with his men
He went without delay.
Richard, the noble and valiant earl,
Straightway surrendered the city to him.

Dublin King Henry gave
To the custody of Hugh de Lacy,
And he afterwards guarded the city
By the command of the king.
And the king of England

Thence turned towards Munster,
To the city of Cashel
Went the king with his splendid following,
Where at that time was the seat
Of the archbishopric of Munster.

From Cashel the puissant king
Went on to Lismore.
King Henry Curt Mantel
At Lismore wished to fortify
A castle: so wished King Henry,

Who was the empress' son.
I know not why, but nevertheless
At this time he put it off.
Towards Leinster the English king
Set out at this time:

Towards Leinster, the rich,
He went with his chivalry.
Eighteen weeks, nor more nor less,
According to what the old people say,
The duke of Normandy remained

In Ireland with his baronage.
Of Normandy at this time
The rich king was duke;
Of Gascony and of Brittany
Of Poitou, of Anjou, and of Maine,

Was King Henry called
Lord, according to the old people.
In Ireland was the king
About a fortnight and four months.
In the land up and down

Marched the noble king.
Victuals were very dear
Throughout all Leinster,
For no provisions came to them
From any other region.

At Dublin was King Henry,
And at Kildare the noble earl.
There the earl abode
With as many men as he had.
While the renowned king

Was in the city of Dublin,
Lo! a messenger in haste
Came in haste from England.
Lo! a messenger
Came to announce to the king

That Henry, his eldest son,
Had in truth revolted against him,
And that he sought to deprive him wholly
Of the lordship of Normandy.
Then the king summoned

Hugh de Lacy, first of all,
And his earls and his vassals
And his free-born barons.
The rich king then gave
The custody of the city of Dublin

And of the castle and the keep
To the baron Hugh de Lacy,
And Waterford, on the other hand,
To the baron Robert the son of Bernard.
The son of Stephen at this juncture

Was left at Dublin,
And Meiler the son of Henry
And Miles the son of David;
With Hugh these were left
By the command of King Henry.

Before that, at this juncture,
The king left Dublin,
To Hugh de Lacy he granted
All Meath in fee
Meath the warrior granted

For fifty knights
Whose service the baron should let him have
Whenever he should have need of it.
To one John he granted Ulster,
If he could conquer it by force;

John de Courcy was his name,
Who afterwards suffered many a trouble there.
Then the king went away to the port,
Towards the city of Wexford;
He made all the master mariners

Get ready his ships.
But Richard the renowned earl
Went to the city of Ferns.
There he married his daughter;
To Robert de Quency he gave her.

There the marriage took place
In the presence of all the baronage.
To Robert de Quency he gave her,
And all the Duffry also,
The constableship of Leinster,

And the standard and the banner.
Here I shall leave off about the earl
And return to my subject;
I would wish, my lords,—know in sooth—
To speak of the rich King Henry.

The king tarried by the sea
At Wexford in order to cross over.
The noble king then crossed over
And landed at Porth'stinian.
With him crossed over the good Milo

And many a vassal and many a baron.
At half a league from St. Davids
King Henry landed;
And the king towards Normandy
Went with his great nobles

In order to make war against a son of his
Who wished to despoil him.
War had the rich king
With the French in Normandy.
In Ireland remained

The noble earl with his friends.
At Kildare he stayed
With all the forces he had.
Often he entered Offaly

In order to plunder O'Dempsey.
O'Dempsey was then called
Lord and defender of Offaly.
The earl entered Offaly
With all his chivalry
In order to spoil and plunder

O'Dempsey, who was so bold,
In that he did not deign to parley with the earl,
Nor would deliver hostages to him.
O'Dempsey then, i'faith,
Would not make peace with the earl.

O'Dempsey with his men
Very bravely, of a truth,
Contended against the earl,
To whom Leinster belongs.
When the earl with his followers

Had entered Offaly,
He then plundered the territory
And sought for cattle in wood and plain.
When he had collected
The spoil from all the district,

To Kildare returned
The renowned English barons.
The earl was ahead in front
With a thousand fighting men;
The constable remained behind

With the rear-guard.
Right at the exit from the pass
He fell upon them very quickly,
O'Dempsey fell upon them,
And the Irish of Offaly.

All the Irish of the district
Attacked the rear-guard.
That day, in short, was slain
The noble Robert de Quency,
Who held the standard and the pennon

Of the region of Leinster,
And to whom the earl had given
The constableship in heritage.
Greatly was he regretted, know in sooth,
The baron Robert de Quency,

And in very great grief
For his death was his good lord.
When this Robert was slain
They buried him honourably.
Robert, who was so noble,

Had indeed a daughter
By his wife, of a truth,
According to the old people;
And she was afterwards given to a baron,
Philip de Prendergast was his name,

The son of Maurice of Ossory,
Who afterwards lived in Hy Kinsellagh.
Concerning this Philip I shall leave off,
Of the noble earl I wish to speak,
And of a brave knight,

Raymond le Gros I heard him called,—
How this baron of great worth
Besought the earl for his sister,
That he should give her to him to wife
And as his friend and consort

With all the constableship
Of Leinster, the rich,
Until the infant should be of an age
To be able to hold her inheritance,
The daughter of Robert de Quency,

Of whom you have already heard,
Or until she should be given
And married to some man
Who could direct the banner
And the standard of Leinster.

The noble earl replied
That he was not advised
To grant the petition
Which the baron had made of him.
Then Raymond departed

He and all his companions;
He took leave of the earl
Very suddenly in evil humour;
To Wales, in short, he then crossed over
Through the anger that he felt

For the earl, in that he had refused
The request he had made.
Thus in such manner
Raymond departed from the country.
He crossed over the sea to Wales,

To Carew Castle he went to dwell.
Concerning Raymond le Gros I shall here leave off
About the English king I shall tell you,
How he sent by messenger—
He announced to the earl

In Ireland by messenger
That he should come to his aid
Speedily in Normandy,
For he was in great perplexity
To govern his territory

And to protect his country
Against the young king his son.
And the earl of great worth,
In order to aid his lord
Crossed the sea to Normandy

And brought a number of knights.
In Ireland he left
Knights serjeants and foot soldiers
In order to conquer the land,
So that the light-footed people of that country,

Who were all his enemies,
Should not be able to annoy him.
When the noble earl
Had come into the presence
Of King Henry Curt-Mantel

Very joyful was the king.
Then the king delivered to him
The city of Gisors in custody;
And the earl with great courtesy
Replied to his lord

That willingly, i'faith,
As long as it should be his pleasure—
He would, in fact, guard the city
As long as the noble king should please.
Such good service did the earl perform

For his lord, King Henry,
That the king, without pretence,
Was well pleased with his service.
The rich king, at his request
To return to Ireland,

Gave leave to the warrior
To return to Ireland.
The king, quit-claimed Wexford
To the earl at this time;
He gave him the custody of the coast

Both Waterford and Dublin.
Then the king caused to be summoned
All the noble knights,
As many as he had at Waterford,
At Dublin and at Wexford,

To come to him
Speedily at his command.
The noble earl, know in sooth,
In such manner departed;
Then he put to sea

And towards Ireland sails:
The noble earl, the warrior,
Sails over the high sea.
By sea he ran
Until he came to Dublin.

Then earl Richard sent word
To the baron Robert the son of Bernard,
And to all the liege barons
Who acknowledged themselves the king's men
Of the city of Waterford,

To knights, barons, and followers,
And to each baron separately,
That by the king's command
All should cross the sea
To aid the king in Normandy.

And the earl again
Sent to Wexford by letter,
Sent word to the barons similarly
On the part of the king Curt-Mantel,
That they should cross over without delay

To succour the king in Normandy.
The son of Stephen also
Crossed the sea to King Henry,
And Maurice of Ossory,
Who afterwards lived in Hy Kinsellagh.

And Hugh de Lacy, who was so bold,
In order to plant his lands,
Set out to Meath
With many a renowned vassal.
Of this Hugh I will say no more,

Of the liege barons I will give you an account.
When the barons had crossed over
Straight to Druidston Chins,
Towards London they turned direct
With all their men.

At this time there was, you must know, a great war
Throughout all England;
For the rich king of Scotland
Was at war with the English king,
And the earl of Leicester then,

According to the statement of the old people,
Had revolted against his lord
And had brought over Flemings.
He thought by their war
To ravage all England,

While the son of the Empress
Warred against his son in Normandy.
Now the vassals and barons
Of the region of England
Encountered the Flemings

At the city of St. Edmunds.
There they were discomfited
And the earl of Leicester taken.
They were discomfited in this manner
By the aid of Leinster,

And by the might of the Irish
The field remained with the English.
And in his turn within that month
The king was taken and conquered.
And the barons of Ireland,

Who were in this brawl,
All passed over to Normandy
And told the news to the king,
How the Flemings were slain
And the king of Scotland taken.

'Ha!' said the king, 'Praise thee, God,
Who art Father and Creator,
For having done me this favour
That my traitors are taken!'
Hear, my lords, valiant barons,

May God of Heaven protect you!
Concerning the English king I shall leave off,
Who was so very noble and brave,
Of the noble earl I will speak
And of his reverses treat:

How the noble earl
Throughout Ireland up and down
Marched, you must know, with his bold men,
Throughout all Leinster.
Then the earl dispatched

A certain interpreter of his,
To Raymond le Gros he sent word
That he should come at once to parley with him,
That the noble earl
Would give him his sister to wife.

Then Raymond equipped himself,
With many a brave vassal.
At Wexford they landed,
According to the history, with three ships.
Then Raymond to Gros sent

To the earl by a lad,
Who told him all the facts:
How Raymond had landed,
And that the earl should speedily
Declare his will to the baron.

The noble earl at this time
Was at the city of Waterford;
To Raymond he sent word
That he would do all his will;
He sent back word also

That to the Isle of Inis-Teimhne
To meet him in parley
Raymond should come with his men.
Accordingly Raymond got ready,
He and all his companions,

To the isle he went
As the earl had directed;
And the earl also
Came there with a very fine suite.
The noble earl of great worth

Brought there his sister then.
There they held a parley,
The earl and the strong-limbed baron,
About marrying his sister;
To Raymond le Gros he will give her.

Thence they set out straightway
To Wexford fighting their way.
There the earl brought his sister,
To Raymond le Gros he then gave her,
Together with the standard and the banner

Of all Leinster,
Until the infant should be of age
To be able to hold her inheritance,
The daughter of Robert de Quency
Of whom you have already heard.

But afterwards a vassal took her,
Philip, a free-born baron,
De Prendergast he was called,
An illustrious liege baron.
This man was such, know ye all,

That in the morning he was peevish and irritable,
But after eating, generous and good tempered,
Courteous and liberal to all.
As soon as he had put on his cloak
He was every day swoln with anger;

But once he had dined in the morning
Then was not a merrier soul under heaven.
This man for a long time
Held the constableship, according to the people,
Very renowned he was,

And loved by everybody,
Very courageous too he was,
And of very great prowess.
Concerning him I will not here relate,
To my subject I will return.

I will tell you my lords of a noble baron,
Of Raymond le Gros I wish to speak,
How the warrior earl
Gave him his sister to wife,
The Forth the earl gave him

In marriage with his sister;
Afterwards he gave him, you must know,
All Odrone in fee,
And Glascarrig also
On the sea towards the east.

He gave Obarthy on the sea,
To Hervey de Mont Maurice.
To Maurice de Prendergast
The valiant earl Richard
Had already given Fernegenal

And in his council confirmed it
Before the renowned earl
Had landed in Ireland;
Ten fiefs he gave him on this condition
For the service of ten knights.

In Fernegenal he dwelt altogether
So that Maurice had him for next neighbour.
I know not how but Robert Fitz Godibert
Held it afterwards, you must know.
Carbury he gave to the good Meiler

Who was such a noble lord.
The earl Richard next gave
To Maurice the son of Gerald—
The Naas the good earl gave
To the son of Gerald with all the honour:

This is the land of Offelan
Which belonged to the traitor MacKelan.
He gave him too Wicklow,
Between Bray and Arklow:
This was the land of Killmantain

Between Ath-cliath and Loch Garman
Twenty fiefs in Omurethy
The noble earl in the same way
Gave to the warrior
Walter de Riddlesford;

To John de Clahull the marshalship
Of Leinster, the rich,
With all the land, know in sooth,
Between Oboy and Leighlin;
To Robert de Birmingham

Offaly to the west of Offelan.
To Adam de Hereford likewise
He gave a rich fief.
And to Miles the son of David,
Who was so intimate with him,

Owerk in Ossory
He gave him as his share.
To Thomas the Fleming he gave
Ardrie, in the presence of his baronage.
Offelimy on the sea

The earl gave to a knight:
To Gilbert de Boisrohard
The earl gave it as his share.
The noble earl, who was so bold,
Gave fifteen fiefs on the sea

To a brave knight,
Reinaud I heard him called.
The Earl Richard the son of Gilbert
Gave Narragh to one Robert.
Who was afterwards indeed killed

In Connaught by his enemies.
In such manner the renowned earl
Divided and gave his land.
Concerning the noble earl I shall here leave off,
Of Hugh de Lacy I shall tell you,

How he enfeoffed his barons,
Knights, serjeants, and retainers.
Castle Knock, in the first place, he gave
To Hugh Tyrrell, whom he loved so much;
And Castle Brack, according to the writing,

To baron William le Petit,
Magheradernon likewise
And the land of Rathkenny;
The cantred of Ardnorcher then
To Meiler, who was of great worth,

Gave Hugh de Lacy—
To the good Meiler Fitz Henry;
To Gilbert de Nangle, moreover,
He gave the whole of Morgallion;
To Jocelin he gave the Navan,

And the land of Ardbraccan,
(The one was son, the other father,
According to the statement of the mother);
To Richard Tuite likewise
He gave a rich fief;

Rathwire he gave moreover
To the baron Robert de Lacy;
To Richard de la Chapelle
He gave good and fine land;
To Geoffrey de Constantine Kilbixi (?)

Near to Rathconarty;
And Skreen he then gave by charter:
To Adam de Phepoe he gave it;
To Gilbert de Nugent,
And likewise to William de Musset,

He gave lands and honours,
In the presence of barons and vavassours;
And to the baron Hugh de Hussey
He then gave fair lands;
To Adam Dullard likewise

The land of 'Rathenuarthi'.
To one Thomas de Craville
He gave in heritage
Emlagh Beccon in quiet enjoyment,
At the north east of Kells,

Laraghcalyn likewise,
And Shanonagh, according to the people,
Gave Hugh de Lacy,
Know in sooth, to this Thomas.
Crandone (?) then to a baron,

Richard the Fleming was his name—
Twenty fiefs he gave him of a truth,
If the geste does not deceive you.
A fortress this man erected
In order to harass his enemies,

Knights and a goodly force he kept there
Archers, serjeants, likewise.
In order to destroy his enemies;
Often he brought them from bad to worse.
But afterwards there came against him O'Carroll,

Who was king of Uriel,
And the rebel MacDunlevy
Of the region of Ulster;
O'Rourke was there, also,
And the king Melaghlin.

Full twenty thousand at this time
Of the Irish came upon them.
Very fiercely they attacked them,
And the barons defended themselves
So long as they could have

Defence in the fortress;
But the Irish from all sides
Hurled their javelins and their darts.
The fortress indeed they destroyed
And slew the garrison within;

But many were previously slain
Of the Irish of the northern districts.
In such manner, know ye all,
Was the country planted
With castles and with cities,

With keeps and with strongholds.
Thus well rooted were
The noble renowned vassals.
And the earl had already conquered
His enemies of Leinster:

For he had with him Murtough,
And next Donnell Kavanagh,
Mac Donachadh and Mac Dalwy,
O'More and O'Dempsey,
O'Duvegan the hoary old man,

Likewise O'Brien of the Duffry,
Gilmoholmock and MacKelan,
And O'Lorcan of Obarthy;
And all the hostages of renown,
The noblest of Leinster,

The earl, you must know, had with him,
According to the ancient custom.
Then Hugh de Lacy
Fortified a house at Trim,
And threw a trench around it,

And then enclosed it with a stockade.
Within the house he then placed
Brave knights of great worth;
Then he entrusted the castle
To the wardenship of Hugh Tyrrel;

To the harbour he went in order to cross
The high seas to England.
But when the king of Connaught heard it—
He who was king at this epoch—
That Hugh had fortified a castle,

He was enraged at the tidings;
His host he summoned to him,
He will go to attack the castle.
All at once O'Connor,
The proud king of Connaught,

Led with him O'Flaherty,
Mac Dermot and Mac Geraghty,
O'Kelly, king of Hy Many,
O'Hart (?) and O'Finaghty,(?)
O'Carbery and O'Flannagan,

And then next O'Monaghan,
O'Dowd and O'Monaghan,
O'Shaughnessy of 'Poltilethban';
King Melaghlin went also,
And his neighbour king O'Rourke,

O'Malory (?) of the Kinel O'Neill,
And likewise Mac Dunlevy;
King O'Carroll went also,
And Mac Tierney(?), who was so base,
Mac Scelling and Mac Artan,

And the rebel Mac Garaghan;
Mackelan likewise
Went with all his men;
O'Neill, the king of the Kinel Owen,
Brought with him three thousand Irish.

The Northerners were assembled,
And all the kings of Leath-Cuinn,
Towards Trim they set out marching
To demolish the castle.
And the baron Hugh Tyrrell

Sent to the earl
A page at full speed
On a very swift horse,
And he told the earl
All the tidings by word of mouth:

How the Northerners were assembled
And all the kings of Leath-Cuinn
To throw down the keep
The castle and the stockade.
'Through me the baron sends you word—

Old Hugh Tyrrell of Trim—
That you aid him in every way,
And succour him with your force.'
And the earl promised him
By word of mouth that he would aid him.

He caused all his men to be summoned
Throughout Leinster speedily.
When they were all assembled,
Old and young, ruddy and fair,
Towards Trim they resolved to march

To encounter the Northerners.
But before the noble earl
Arrived with his men,
Hugh had of a truth
Utterly abandoned his charge,

Because he was not in sufficient force
Within the castle nor without
To offer fight or combat
Without the help of the earl.
When the English were gone

And had abandoned their house,
The Irish arrived at Trim.
Their numbers I shall by no means tell,
How many they were nor what thousands,
For I should be thought to be lying.

The rampart they threw completely down
And levelled it even with the ground,
But first of all they put
The house to flames.
When they had accomplished their work

They retreated altogether:
They made a show of returning
To their country, the wicked tyrants.
And the earl, who was so bold,
To Trim resolved to hasten

To protect the house,
If he could arrive in time.
To Trim the earl went with all speed
And with him many a valiant vassal.
But when the earl had arrived,

By the river he then alighted;
For he found there standing
Neither house nor cabin, big or little,
Within which he could take his ease
And lodge for that night.

Then the earl made proclamation
And commanded throughout the host,
That all should straightway mount.
Then he threw himself on his horse
And set off on the straight road

Pursuing at a great pace.
So much did the earl exert himself
That he came up with the rear;
He charged them speedily
Without any pause;

And the Irish who had no armour
Then scattered themselves
By sevens and eights, by threes and fours,
So that they did not hold together.
And the earl then slew

Of these men seven score and ten.
Then, you must know, he made a retreat
To Dublin with great confidence,
And Hugh Tyrrell went to Trim
And re-fortified his fortress;

After that he guarded it with great honour
Until the arrival of his lord.
And the earl throughout Leinster
Went marching back and forwards,
Until he resolved

That he would at length march
Against King Donnell O'Brien
With the advice of his English.
His host he summons, all at once,
The strongest of Leinster,

That all should be in attendance,
Old and young, small and great.
At the banner and the pennon
Of the constable Raymond le Gros.
My lords, may God befriend you!

Knights, serjeants, and attendants,
I will tell you of a knight,
Raymond le Gros I heard him called,
A valiant baron he was,
A vassal daring and victorious,

Very rich and powerful he was,
And the most puissant of his peers.
Constable is Raymond
Of the province of Leinster.
Knights he retained and a goodly force

By the earl's command,
Knights he had and common soldiers,
Archers, serjeants, and fighting-men,
To put to shame and outlawry
The Irish enemies of the king.

Hearken, my lords and worthy folk,
If ye would hear now plainly:
Of a knight I will tell you,
A baron, a noble warrior,
Of the constable Raymond le Gros,

How he summons his host from all quarters
Up and down throughout the land,
Through Meath and through Leinster,
All the esquirehood
Well armed and well equipped,

Knights, serjeants, and common soldiers,
With army equipped and ready;
To meet Raymond in Ossory
The baronage should come,
And he will have them guided forward

Against King O'Brien, who was so bold.
The Irish king of Ossory
Will go in their company,
And he will truly lead the host, so he said,
And guide it against King O'Brien,

As far as the city of Limerick
He will guide it in safety.
Why should I go on telling you more,
Either more or less, little or much?
When the host had assembled,

Towards Munster they then turned;
And the king of Ossory
Guides them forward in the van:
Towards Munster he guided them,
Against King O'Brien he brought this host.

But Raymond, according to the people,
Did not trust him entirely
Before that he had assured him,
Pledged his faith and sworn,
That he would never commit any deceit

Nor treason nor treachery of any kind
Against him or his men henceforward.
And the king at once
Said to him then in the presence of all:
'You will be wrong to doubt it;

Nay, I will guide you quite right,
And I shall pledge you my word.'
When the king had said this,
They march forward, without gainsaying,
They march all night and the next day,

Now in woods, now in the open,
Until they came to a renowned city
Which was named Limerick.
This city was surrounded
By a river, a wall, and a dyke,

So that no man could pass over
Without a ship or a bridge,
Neither in winter nor in summer,
Except by a difficult ford.
There passed over first that day

The baron Meiler the son of Henry.
Wherefore it was well said:
'We shall call it Meiler's ford';
For when the host of Leinster
Came to Limerick in this way,

To the river they came
So that they were going to return without more;
When a knight of St. David's
Who was brought up in this land,
Meiler the son of Henry was his name,

With a loud voice raises a cry:
The son of Henry, the baron Meiler,
Began to call aloud:
To the front he went shouting,
'Pass over, knights: why do ye tarry?'

Into the river he straightway threw himself,
And his white horse bears him across.
When the knight had crossed over
'St. David!' he shouted loud and clear.
For he was his lord

Under the Lord God the Creator.
And the knight with great affection
Invoked St. David night and day,
That he might aid him
In doing deeds of valour;

That he should give him strength, and praise, and renown
Against all his enemies.
Often he invoked St. David,
That he should not leave him in forgetfulness,
But give him might and vigour

In the midst of his enemies that day.
After him there crossed over
Many barons and knights well armed.
Before they had all crossed over
Many were drowned that day.